QUATIE ROSS

First Lady of the Cherokee Nation

Dorothy Audrey Simpson, Ed. D.

HERITAGE BOOKS
2018

HERITAGE BOOKS
AN IMPRINT OF HERITAGE BOOKS, INC.

Books, CDs, and more—Worldwide

For our listing of thousands of titles see our website
at
www.HeritageBooks.com

Published 2018 by
HERITAGE BOOKS, INC.
Publishing Division
5810 Ruatan Street
Berwyn Heights, Md. 20740

Copyright © 2017 Dorothy Audrey Simpson, Ed. D.

Heritage Books by the author:
*From Pajarito to Lungchow: Memoirs of
Photographic Reconnaissance Pilot Stanley A. Hardin*
Quatie Ross: First Lady of the Cherokee Nation

All rights reserved. No part of this book may be reproduced or transmitted in any form or by any means, electronic or mechanical, including photocopying, recording or by any information storage and retrieval system without written permission from the author, except for the inclusion of brief quotations in a review.

International Standard Book Number
Paperbound: 978-0-7884-5781-4

TABLE OF CONTENTS

CHAPTER

Page

1. Growing Up in the Land of "The Real People" — 1
2. The Story of Quatie's People — 7
3. Losses — 13
4. Wife of a Chief — 19
5. Chief John Ross, "The Indian Prince" — 25
6. The "First Lady" of the Cherokees — 37
7. Peaceful Protests — 45
8. "The Place Where They Cried" — 59
9. A Mother's Love — 65
10. A Soldier's Midnight Vigil — 69
11. A New Hope — 73

APPENDIX — 79

BIBLIOGRAPHY — 83

CHAPTER 1

Growing Up in the Land of "The Real People"

Over two hundred years ago, a baby girl was born in a part of the United States known as the Cherokee Nation. The girl's name was Elizabeth Brown. Just as many children today are given nick-names, Elizabeth was given the name "Quatie." She would grow up to be a wife, a mother, and a helper to her husband, Chief of the Cherokees. She would be the First Lady of the Cherokee Nation.

Born in the year 1791, Quatie came into the world in what is now the state of Tennessee, probably at Ooltewah, Tennessee. At that time the Cherokees lived in the southern Appalachian Mountains.

We cannot be sure of the names of Quatie's parents. So much time has passed that her mother's name seems to have been lost. Her father was probably James Brown, the Treasurer of the Cherokee Nation. Quatie was a full blood Cherokee of the Bird Clan.

Knowing something about where Quatie grew up and how the Cherokee people lived will help us to understand the kind of girl Quatie was. When Columbus discovered America in 1492, he thought at first that he was in India, so he called the native people he met "Indians." The name stuck, and from then on, the Native Americans were often referred to as "American Indians" or simply as "Indians." There were many tribes. The Cherokees were among the largest and most progressive of all the tribes.

The Cherokees called themselves Ani-Yun' Wiua, or "The Real People." The word "Cherokee" came later from the Choctaw Chillaki and means "cave dweller." The Cherokees lived in the Southern Allegheny and Great Smoky Mountains.

The Cherokees first encountered the European or so-called "white" culture when Hernando de Soto and his soldiers visited their lands in 1540. Later, many English and Scottish settlers and traders were welcomed by the friendly Cherokee people. Many of the white people and the Cherokee people became good friends. Some of them married.

In the early days, the Cherokees lived in sixty-four towns with about 300 people in each town. There were seven sacred mother towns, each populated by as many as 600 people. Kituwah, near the present-day Bryson City, North Carolina, was the oldest of all the towns. It may have been the Cherokee's first permanent settlement after their migration from the Great Lakes area to the Southeastern part of the United States. When Quatie was a little girl, the Cherokees were the largest tribe in the Southeast. About twenty thousand Cherokees lived in what are now the states of Georgia, Tennessee, Alabama, Kentucky, Virginia, North Carolina and South Carolina.

In 1821, a Cherokee named Sequoya found a way to write down the Cherokee language. He developed an alphabet so that the Cherokee people could learn to read and write in their own language. The Cherokees had their own schools and their own postal system. They even had their own newspaper. It was called the *Cherokee Phoenix* and was established in 1828 at New Echota, the capital of the Cherokee Nation. Many of the Cherokees learned of the white man's religion and became Christians. They built Christian churches. They also built schools and houses, planted fields and orchards, and had herds of beef. They manufactured cloth. They built roads. They operated taverns and ferries. They had a system of laws which were enforced by peace officers and native courts.

In 1828, the Cherokee Nation adopted a written constitution and established a government with a legislature, courts, and an executive branch, modeled after the white people's system with its legislative, judicial, and executive branches of government. The Cherokee Constitution was approved or ratified on July 4, 1827. The Fourth of July was selected for the important date as a gesture of courtesy and admiration for the big sister Republic of the United States of America. No other Indian tribe had ever created a formal government like this, one with such highly structured written laws.

So this is the world where Elizabeth Brown, "Quatie", was born. It was a world where the Cherokee culture and the white culture met and lived together in peace for a time. But the peace between the two races was short lived. Years before Quatie was born, the new-comers, known as white people, began to want the land of the Cherokees for themselves. They wanted the Cherokee people to leave their land and move to the west.

The Cherokee people believed that their land was sacred. They had great respect for the land. They had a deep belief that the land in the west was an evil region while the land in the east, where they lived, was the good land. So the Cherokees had an especially strong desire to remain on their lands in the east. They did not want to move west to an unknown land. Some Cherokees said they would rather die than move to the evil west.

Yet the white people began to push for more Indian land. The problems the Cherokee people faced when dealing with their white neighbors became more and more difficult, but the Cherokees tried to carry on their lives as they had in the past. As Quatie grew, she helped her mother with the household chores. She probably carried water to be used for washing dishes. Water was heated on wood stoves for washing. There was no electricity, no running water, no indoor bathroom, no central heating. Wood stoves were used for cooking and for heat. Candles or lamps were used for light. Clothes were not bought ready-made at the store. They were made at home by hand-stitching. The house had to be cleaned. The clothes had to be washed by hand. The meals had to be cooked on wood stoves after fires had been built up by putting wood into the stoves. Many things were made by hand, including soap, candles, clothes, and toys. While the men were out working in the fields, the women and children did the household chores. Quatie must have been proud as she learned to do more and more things for her mother.

Quatie learned to read and write. Many children in those days did not, but Quatie's parents thought it was important for a little girl to learn to read. She learned in both her native language, Cherokee, and in English. By the time she was eight or ten years of age, she could read and write in two languages quite well. Of course she could speak both languages fluently. Although the Cherokee people continued to observe the old traditions, many of them accepted the white man's religion and became Christians. Quatie was Christian and belonged to the Moravian Church.

An important event took place in the Cherokee year in September. The time for the Feast of the Green Corn, by the ancient calendar, was celebrated in the month of the seventh moon which was called Maize. The purpose of the Feast was to give thanks for the harvest and to rekindle the sacred fire. On the third day of the celebration, a wonderful feast was prepared by the women while the children played near the cabins or in the nearby fields.

The sacred fire was kindled. As the flames crackled, the women came and took back coals to their cabins to rekindle the old fires. Then the feasting began. Perhaps Quatie helped her mother prepare the freshly baked bread, ripe corn roasted in the husk and rich meat stews. In the evening, the elders would tell ghost stories around the fire, many of them about the spirits of the animals who lived in their lands. One story was called "the

Raven Mocker." It was about a raven which swooped down on dark wings to steal the souls of the dying. The children always listened to these stories intently.

In spite of the fact that the Cherokees tried to live as they had lived for generations on those same lands, the white people continued hoping to obtain Cherokee lands for themselves. Some of the white men were greedy and cruel, willing to do anything to get the land they wanted.

Growing up in the land of "The Real People" was not easy for Elizabeth Brown, the little Cherokee girl called Quatie. Not only were the Cherokees in danger of losing their lands, but they were in danger of losing their very lives.

CHAPTER 2

The Story of Quatie's People

The white people began to push for more Indian land. In 1642, the House of Burgesses in England passed an act which gave explorers the right to discover and explore the western part of the country in the new land. After that, the Virginia colonists began to look westward.

In 1721, the Cherokees met with the Charlestown Governor, Francis Nicholson. They agreed to name a single head man with whom the colonists could negotiate. The Cherokees agreed to trade only with the English, to allow no other whites in their country, and to turn any law-breakers escaping to their country over to the British. At that time, the Cherokees made their first cession of land to the whites, a small strip on the Carolina border. In return, the British offered protection and friendship "for as long as the mountains and rivers last and the sun shines."

Soon missionaries came and established schools. Moravian, Baptist, and Presbyterian missionaries opened mission schools. Many Cherokees were happy to learn about Jesus Christ, the Savior of the World. More and more Cherokees became Christians and began to learn the ways of the white man.

One of many problems brought by Europeans to the Indians was the introduction of certain diseases which had been unknown to the Native Americans before. In 1738, the Cherokees were stricken by smallpox.

Smallpox caused the deaths of half of the entire population of the Cherokee nation in less than a year. Unlike the Europeans, the Cherokees had no resistance to smallpox, as it was entirely new to them.

The Cherokees were just recovering from a smallpox epidemic when the French and Indian War broke out in 1754. The Cherokees had already agreed to side with the British, so they allied themselves with the English colonists. Sometimes, however, the English soldiers could not tell the difference between their Indian allies and their Indian enemies. So at times the British killed their Cherokee friends along with their enemies.

In 1775, the Cherokee nation lost more land. The Treaty of Parish, which was the final settlement of the French and Indian War, gave England title or ownership to all American lands east of the Mississippi. In order to open up the frontier to white settlement, white men determined that the Indians were "to be disposed," by treaty if possible or, if that failed, then by warfare. The Cherokees found themselves at Sycamore Shoals negotiating a huge land sale.

During the American Revolution, when the American settlers fought for their freedom from British rule, most of the Indian tribes remained neutral in the war of white men against white men. While most Native Americans refused to take sides, about one-fourth of the Cherokees allied with the British to fight the colonists. One of the leaders of that group was the Cherokee named Dragging Canoe, son of Little Carpenter. George Washington, later to become the first President of the United States, was then a lieutenant colonel in the militia. He admired the Cherokees and how well they could fight. He once wrote that the Cherokees were "more serviceable" than two times their number of white men.

In 1776, the same year the Americans declared their independence from the British, many Cherokee towns were devastated. Hundreds of Cherokee people were auctioned off as slaves. In 1785, the Cherokee Nation made a treaty with the new republic of the United States of America. Friendly relations were then established. But the Cherokees lost more land. In return for more lands under the Treaty of Hopewell, the United States Government set the formal boundaries of the Cherokee land. The Treaty stated that the United States would respect the Cherokees' land and that no further white intrusion or interference would be allowed. But whites continued to live on Cherokee lands, even though it was illegal. The U.S. Government did nothing to make the intruders leave.

When Dragging Canoe died in 1792, the new leader was The Ridge (Man Who Walks on Mountain Top). He came to the Council and helped convince the tribe to enter the Creek War of 1812 on the side of the white Americans. (Later The Ridge was called "Major Ridge" because Andrew Jackson gave him that title after the Cherokees helped him win victory.)

Many Native Americans believed the white men were unfair to them in taking their lands. Tecumsch, the great Shawnee chief, came south to urge unity among the Indian tribes. He brought a bundle of red sticks with him to show that divided sticks are easily broken; but when sticks are put together, they are strong. His message was that the Indians should unite for strength. A large group of Creek Indians agreed with him. They declared war on the whites. This group of warring Indians became known as the Red Sticks.

The Creek Red Sticks assaulted Fort Mims in Alabama on August 30, 1813. They murdered 500 white people, mostly women and children. The white people were angry and determined to fight against the Red Sticks. They asked the Cherokees for help. This war put the Cherokees in an unusual situation since the Creeks were their Indian neighbors. But the United States Government demanded that the Cherokees choose sides. So The Real People raised a company of volunteers to fight alongside the white men.

A leader named Andrew Jackson, later to become President of the United States, was at that time in command of the Tennessee militia that gathered against the Creeks. Several hundred Cherokees marched with Jackson. At the Battle of Horseshoe Bend, it was the Cherokee warriors who helped tip the scales in Jackson's favor by defeating the Red Sticks. Jackson's attacks had been unsuccessful until March 28, 1814. At that time, Cherokee Chief Junaluska and his warriors made a move that won the battle for Jackson. Junaluska and another Cherokee leader, John Ross, swam the icy waters of the Tallapoosa River with daggers in their teeth. They cut loose the Creek canoes which had been put there for escape. Then they brought those canoes back with them for their own Cherokee allies to use in a rear attack on the Creeks. This unexpected plan diverted the attention of the Creeks, so Jackson was able to storm the entrenchments in front. The victory was a big step toward putting General Jackson in the White House. Andrew "Andy" Jackson, often called "Old Hickory," owed his success to the help of the clever Cherokees, one of whom was John Ross. Yet in time he would betray Ross and his Cherokee people.

While the Cherokee volunteers were helping win the war for the whites, the white settlers were plundering Cherokee lands, selling their livestock, destroying their crops, and setting fire to their villages. Afterward, Jackson demanded 23 million acres of Creek Land, but he also tried to include some of the Cherokee's Tennessee land, even though the Cherokees had helped him win his victory. When the Cherokees refused to give him the land, Jackson tried bribery. He received a small land cession in the treaty he negotiated in 1817. This was only the beginning of more and more attempts by white officials to gain Cherokee land.

The world into which Quatie was born was a world of conflict between so-called white men and so-called red men. It was a world in which the white men wanted to expand westward across the continent, pushing the red man ever west. But the Cherokees did not want to give up their land in the east to move to the dark land of the "evil" west. The Cherokees declared more than once that not another single foot of soil would ever be sold. But by 1827, the whites were putting more pressure on the Cherokees to turn over more land to them. The Real People began to worry that the white man might push them westward in spite of everything.

CHAPTER 3

Losses

Elizabeth Brown, "Quatie," grew up in a comfortable home and obtained a good education. She married at a young age and had a child by the time she was 21. Quatie was very young when she fell in love with a Mr. Henley. Not much is known about Quatie's first husband. Even his first name seems to have eluded historians, although some have given his name as Martin Henley. Before she was 21, Quatie gave birth to a daughter named Susan. The Henleys were delighted with their baby daughter.

But shortly after the birth of his daughter Susan, Mr. Henley died. Elizabeth "Quatie" Brown Henley was little more than a girl herself when she became a widow with a young child. Some historians say Quatie and Mr. Henley had two children, but most records list only Susan. Perhaps there was another child that died at birth.

As Quatie tried to get over her sorrow following her husband's death, she became the object of attention of another young man. Who was the young man wishing to win the heart of the young widow, Quatie Henley? Her new suitor was John Ross, the well-known leader of the Cherokee nation. In 1813, John Ross and Quatie were married. Quatie was just 22 years old. Her new husband was 23.

When she married John Ross, Quatie may have sensed that her husband would play an important role in her nation's destiny. At the age of

23, when John married Quatie, he was already a leader among his people. Even before he was 20, John had been sent on several important missions requiring leadership abilities.

The conflicts between Indians and whites, Indians and Indians, and whites and whites had left the Cherokee nation in a turmoil it had never known before. Undoubtedly, Quatie, like the other people, looked to their leaders for wisdom and guidance.

Following the War of 1812, two Cherokee leaders, John Ross and Major Ridge, visited President James Madison to read the requests of the Cherokee Nation aloud. They wanted the U.S. Government to remove white intruders from Cherokee land. They had other requests as well, such as obtaining pensions for wounded Cherokee victims of the war. Their requests were granted. In return, the Cherokees gave the United States the right to build roads through Cherokee Territory. They also sold a small triangle of land in South Carolina to the U. S. Government for five thousand dollars. Ross and the others were pleased with their agreement because they thought that the boundaries of the Cherokee Nation were fixed forever. They thought they had convinced President Madison that their people would never migrate to the west.

But the Cherokee leaders were wrong. The U.S. Government still wanted the Cherokees to exchange their eastern land for western land. Andrew Jackson, called "Old Sharp Knife" by some, was one of three commissioners sent by President Monroe to make a new treaty with the Cherokee Nation. John Ross and his brother-in-law, Elijah Hicks, were appointed to reply to the U.S. Government's demands. They drew up a statement that the Cherokees wished "to remain in the land of our fathers without further cession of territory." Hicks gave the statement to Jackson after 69 chiefs had signed it.

But Jackson had persuaded 22 Cherokees to sign the new treaty he had brought from Washington. But the 22 men were not chiefs! In fact, they had no authority to sign a treaty at all. Under that treaty, the U.S. bought two tracks of land in Georgia and Tennessee. Jackson and the other commissioners offered any Cherokee who emigrated west, a rifle, ammunition, a blanket, and a brass kettle or a beaver trap. Jackson and the other commissioners went back to Washington as if they had a legal treaty, as though the National Council had ratified it. The Cherokees considered it an illegal treaty because the signers were not in authority to act for the Cherokee Nation.

Of fifteen thousand Cherokees, only 700 moved to Arkansas under the terms of Jackson's "treaty." Less than a hundred years since the Cherokees had made their first treaty with the British, over one-half of their lands were gone. In the years from 1798 to 1819, twenty-four separate land cessions had been taken from them. The U.S. Commissioners again came for land in 1822, spreading bribes as they went. Even the leader John Ross was offered a large bribe. He refused it.

Gold was discovered on Cherokee land in 1828. To make matters worse, that same year Andrew Jackson was elected President of the United States. Those two events meant trouble for the Cherokees. White men with "gold fever" stampeded into Georgia. President Jackson made it clear that he would not rest until he had taken every inch of Indian land east of the Mississippi. Jackson decided to bring the Cherokee nation to its knees. One of the first things he did was to cut off the six-thousand dollar annuity paid for decades by previous Presidents to the Cherokee's national treasury. This money was payment for the hundreds of thousands of acres of Indian land taken in the past.

When the elderly Chief Junaluska heard of Jackson's plans against the Cherokee nation, he remembered the battle where he had helped his friend "Old Sharp Knife" win the victory. Junaluska said, "If I had known that Jackson would drive us from our homes, I would have killed him that day on the Horseshoe." Instead, he and John Ross had helped make Jackson a war hero, not knowing he would later turn against them. The Cherokees gave Jackson a new nickname. They called him "Chicken Snake" because they considered this creature the most detestable one in nature.

In 1829, when Jackson gave his first State of the Union message, he made it clear that he intended to open up the western states to the white farmers and shopkeepers who had elected him. They were men like those in

Georgia who wanted the Indian land and the gold that had been found on it. President Jackson told Congress that he was introducing the Indian Removal Act, an act which would uproot all the southeastern tribes, including the Cherokees, and move them across the Mississippi to Indian Territory in the west. The dreaded move west loomed like a black cloud above the Cherokee nation.

Eleven days after Jackson's announcement of his Indian Removal Act, the state of Georgia, where gold had been discovered on Cherokee land, passed laws called the Indian Codes. The laws were passed because the State knew that the federal government, under President Jackson's leadership, would not stop them. These laws made the existence of the Cherokees in Georgia intolerable if not impossible.

When Georgia passed its Indian Codes, knowing the new President would not protest against them, the Cherokee Nation was deprived of its human rights. In reality, the Codes declared that the Cherokee Nation no longer existed. The Codes meant that the white men could come in and take the land they wanted. They would push the Cherokees west as they devoured the land for themselves.

Now people like Quatie--who had lived in peace all their lives, trying their best to adapt to the white intruders--had to face an uncertain future. Their people had welcomed the Europeans and learned their language and customs, had embraced their religion and their ideals to a large extent. However, they did not anticipate that the white men would want to buy their land--or take it any way they could. The concept of buying and selling land was not part of the Native American way of thinking but it was a definite part of the European way. Thus, conflict was inevitable.

CHAPTER 4

Wife of a Chief

The young widow, Quatie, found happiness once again in her marriage to John Ross. He was a very busy man but always had his family at heart as he worked for the Cherokee people. In 1828, he helped formulate the Cherokee Constitution. In fact, he wrote much of the Cherokee constitution. Ross had become well-known among the Cherokees for his success in dealing with the white men. When Path Killer died in 1827, John Ross and Major Ridge were the main leaders.

Then John was elected Principal Chief of the Cherokee Nation. Quatie became the First Lady of the Cherokee Nation. As President and First Lady of the Cherokee Nation, John and Quatie Ross lived in a well-furnished, white frame house at the end of the Coosa River in Georgia. The couple was adored by the Cherokee people.

The Ross home was built in 1797. It was surrounded by roses. A pair of peacocks adorned the front lawn. But John did not stay at home as much as he would have liked. He made many trips to Washington, D.C. to try to convince President Monroe that the Cherokee claims to their own land were true and just claims. Later, more trips were made to try to persuade President John Quincy Adams to allow the Cherokees to keep their lands.

Soon after the Indian Codes of Georgia were passed, John Ross led a delegation to Washington, D.C. But he was not allowed to meet with

President Jackson. He and his people waited a full month. Finally, the Secretary of War told them that the only solution was for all Cherokees to move west immediately. The laws of Georgia allowed confiscation of large sections of Cherokee land. This meant that the white men could take away Indian land legally. The Indian Codes made the Cherokee Nation's laws null and void, or meaningless. The laws caused nearly all debts owed to Indians by whites to be cancelled.

Another thing the Indian Codes did was to prohibit any Indian from testifying in court against a white man, no matter what the white man had done to the Indian. On one occasion, two women accused a white man of rape. They wanted to take him to court, but they were not allowed to do so because of the Indian Codes.

Additionally, the new laws provided for the imprisonment of any Indian who even spoke against the planned emigration across the Mississippi to the west. The newly discovered gold fields were taken. The Codes stated that no Indian could take precious metals from Georgia soil, not even from his own backyard. It was unlawful for the Cherokee Council to meet for any purpose except to sign over their land to the United States. Judges were not permitted to hold court in the Cherokee nation. All Cherokee lands were to be surveyed and mapped out into homestead lots of 160 acres and "gold lots" of 40 acres. Then these lands were to be distributed to white citizens of Georgia by a public lottery. Bands of mounted vigilantes called "Pony Clubs" invaded Cherokee lands, killing livestock, setting fires, and committing murders. So in reality, the Georgia Codes made the Cherokees completely helpless under the law no matter how much they were mistreated.

Chief Ross appealed time and again for relief from the Indian Code laws. But Jackson's only message was that the President of the United States had no power to protect them against the laws of Georgia. Still, Ross did not give up. Many Cherokees wanted to rise up against the white men, but Chief Ross argued for peaceful settlement of all disputes. He wanted his people to remain within the law, even if the law was wrong, for he felt that violence would only cause more problems. He told his people to put in their crops, to continue to weave their cloth, to attend the mission services, and to send their children to the mission schools. He assured his people that he and the Council would keep them informed of the affairs of the nation.

After Quatie and John were married, Quatie became the mother of six more children, another girl and five boys. Her life was busy as a wife and mother of seven. Sometimes her health was not good. But Quatie was a very strong woman. It was not easy for her to be the wife of such a busy man, a man whose work was really his mission in life. He was gone from home for long periods of time. Quatie must have spent many lonely hours wondering when the problems her husband Chief John Ross had to confront would be resolved.

Georgia's lottery for Cherokee lands was completed by 1833. More than 500 surveyors on Cherokee lands began cutting them up into segments for the public lottery. Thousands of whites rushed into Cherokee territory to seize the new land they had won in the lottery. Cherokee families were forced out of their homes and driven away.

Chief Ross and his family were no exception. They, too, were victims of the lottery. In April, 1835. Colonel William N. Bishop, head of the Georgia Guard, had tried to reach John in Washington, D.C. to let him know that he had taken legal claim of the Chief's property. John no longer possessed his home, fields, ferry, or livestock.

But Chief Ross did not receive the message before he left Washington. One night, after spending many weeks in Washington trying to reach peaceful agreements with the white leaders, John Ross rode home. He was unaware of the fact that he no longer owned a home. Ross arrived about ten o'clock in the evening.

Ross found a stranger waiting for him in the shadows by his front gate. The man reached out and took hold of the horse's bridle. He told Chief Ross that his name was James Jones. He announced that he, Jones, was the new owner of Ross' horses, livestock, house, and land. John dismounted. For a moment he stood speechless. He must have been shocked and angry. He must have been afraid for his family. After hesitating a moment, Ross hurried into the house where he found his sick wife, Quatie, and their children crowded into two small rooms. The new owner had agreed to let them stay there until the Chief returned to move them out. But the white man's family already occupied the rest of the house.

John gathered up as many of his possessions as the new owner, James Jones, would permit. Chief Ross had to pay Jones to care for a horse that he left on the property. One can only image the shock and dismay that Ross must have felt that evening. In spite of his anger, he knew that fighting at that point would be futile. He undoubtedly tried to comfort his wife and children as they prepared to leave the house that had been their beautiful home.

Chief Ross took his family out of Georgia and across the Tennessee line. There the Ross family sat up housekeeping in a rough one-room log cabin at "Red Hill" or Flint Springs near Red Clay Council Grounds.

It must have been hard for Quatie to move from the beautiful, big home into a cabin with just one room. She must have felt like a displaced monarch, a queen in exile. She, like John, may have been angry at the injustice of the Georgia Codes. The Native Americans under the Indian Codes were not treated like human beings. The attitude of the men who drew up the Georgia Codes was totally alien to men who believed in justice and equality. Yet the Cherokees could do little to change the Codes until reasonable men could be prevailed upon to change them.

All of the Ross children had to get used to living in such little space.

They had been accustomed to better conditions. John and his family lived in the little log cabin until 1838. It was in that year that the real strength of Quatie Ross, John Ross, and the Cherokee Nation was tested.

CHAPTER 5

Chief John Ross, "The Indian Prince"

After Quatie married John Ross, her life was changed by the busy and productive work of her husband. She supported him in every way and taught the children well. Some background on the life of John Ross will serve to show how Quatie's own life changed when she married this extraordinarily devoted young man.

John Ross was one of the greatest of the Cherokee chiefs because he led his people through their most trying and troublesome time, always urging unity, always seeking peace. He never resorted to violence or illegal ways of opposing the whites, even though they continued to cheat the Cherokees out of their land. He believed in finding peaceful ways to settle disagreements.

Born in Marysville, Tennessee, John Ross came into the world on October 3, 1790, the third child of Daniel and Mollie Ross. He was one of nine children. Like Quatie, he had a nick-name. His boyhood name was *Tsan-usdi* or "Little John." (John was named for his father, who was called "Big John.") As a man, John was called *Guwisguwi* or *Cooweescoowee*, (or *Kooweskoowe)* the name of a large white bird or swan or "the Egret." This was a mythological or rare migratory bird, one that must have been much admired by the Cherokees, perhaps for its grace, skill, beauty or strength.

John's father, Daniel Ross, born July 14, 1760 in Sutherlandshire,

Scotland, was the first of the Ross generation in America. He decided to settle among the Cherokees. Daniel Ross married Mary Mollie McDonald in 1786 at Chickamauga, Tennessee. He died May 22, 1830 in Tennessee.

Mary Mollie McDonald, John's mother, was one-quarter Cherokee of the Bird Clan. She was born November 1, 1770, at Fort Loudoun, Tennessee. She was a daughter of John McDonald and Annie Shorey. She died October 5, 1808 at Marysville, Tennessee, after having reared nine children who were one-eighth Cherokee.

Not much is known about John McDonald, the father of Mary Mollie McDonald, (and grandfather of John Ross) except that he was an Englishman and married Annie Shorey in the Cherokee Nation East. It is known that he came to America in hope of economic gain. He was born in the Scottish Highlands at Inverness about 1747. He arrived in America about 1766. He lived for a while in Charleston, South Carolina. Then he worked in Georgia before being commissioned for a trading post at Fort Loundoun on the Georgia-Tennessee frontier. It was probably at Fort Loudoun that John McDonald met Anne Shorey, (grandmother of John Ross.) She was the daughter of an interpreter. In 1769 they married.

Annie Shorey's father was William Shorey, (John Ross' great grandfather). William Shorey was a settler who came from Scotland to live in the Cherokee Nation East, Tennessee. He married a full blood Cherokee of the Bird Clan, *Ghigooioe*. (Great grandmother of John Ross.) Translated in English, *Ghigooie* means "Sweetheart." Little is known about Annie's mother except that she was born in Tennessee and that she and William Shorey had two daughters, Annie and Elizabeth. William Shorey served the British for an interpreter at Fort Loudoun. Because he was fluent in the Cherokee language, Shorey was asked to go with Lieutenant Henry Timberlake and a group of Cherokees to England. But he died during the journey in May of 1762.

There is an interesting story about how John Ross's parents met. After Daniel Ross came to America, he was orphaned at the time the American Revolution ended. He joined a trader named Mr. Mayberry and went with him to Hawkins, Tennessee. There they built a flatboat. They put goods on it for sale in the Chicasaw Nation. But as they passed down the Tennessee River, they were captured by a group of Chickamaugh Indians. (They were Indians who usually killed their captives.) The Chickamaugas had separated themselves from the Cherokee Nation earlier when Little Carpenter and others had signed a treaty in 1775 with the Americans, ending all their lands in Kentucky and middle Tennessee. The group was headed by Little Carpenter's son, Dragging Canoe. They settled on Chickamauga Creek at Chickamauga. There John McDonald, Deputy British Agent to the Chickamaugas, built a cabin and commissary where he kept the Chickamaugas supplied with weapons and ammunition for raiding the American border. (This was when the American Revolutionary War was beginning.) Dragging Canoe had allied himself with the British.

When the Indians brought in their captive, Daniel Ross, it was John McDonald who interceded for his life; and the Indians agreed not to kill their captive. Daniel Ross, who was Scottish like McDonald, was invited to open a trading post in the Cherokee Nation in partnership with John McDonald. Daniel accepted the invitation. Before very long, Daniel and John McDonald's daughter, Molly, fell in love and married.

When the Chickamaugas made peace agreements with the Americans, Daniel Ross and John McDonald built Ross House at Rossville, Georgia in 1797. Daniel Ross established his store on Chattanooga Creek near the foot of Lookout Mountain and operated it there until about 1816.

It can be seen that John Ross, then, came from a line of Scottish and Cherokee ancestors. The third child, he grew up with his six sisters and three brothers in Tennessee. His two older sisters were Jennie, born March 25, 1787, and Elizabeth, born March 25, 1789. He had two little brothers, Lewis, born February 26, 1796, and Andrew, born December 19, 1789. There was a sister born after Lewis. Her name was Susannah. She was born December 10, 1793. The three youngest children were girls: Annie, born November 15, 1800; Margaret, born July 5, 1803; and Maria, born January 13, 1806.

Young John grew up watching the Cherokees who traded at his father's store. John's friends gathered around the store. Many of them were

Cherokee children. John grew to identify more with the Cherokee side of his family than with the white side. He even wanted to dress in the traditional Indian clothing rather than in white American clothing. Perhaps his wish to dress in Indian clothing started when his young Cherokee friends made fun of his American clothing. When he changed into the traditional Indian clothing, they approved. He wanted their approval. So he often wore the Indian clothing to please his Indian friends. Even though John was more white than Indian, he felt in his heart that he was more Cherokee than he was white. He was educated in the white man's ways, but he learned the Cherokee ways as well.

Young John Ross was tutored by white teachers. John's father wanted the very best education for his children. He had a fine library and encouraged his children to read. He employed a teacher, John Barbour Davis, to instruct his children. John's father started the first school in the Rossville and Chattanooga area. When John was older, he went to school at Kingston, Tennessee. There he studied under a Presbyterian minister, the Rev. Gideon Blackburn. Later, he attended the academy at Maryville, Tennessee. John was involved in his studies there when, at the age of 18, he learned that his mother had died at the Ross House on October 5, 1808. She was 39 years of age. She died just two years after her last child had been born. John was stricken with grief, but undoubtedly his faith sustained him.

John was not the kind of youth one might think would attain success as a great Indian leader. He was slight of stature and of medium build. He had dark brown hair. John, being fair, did not look like his dark-skinned Cherokee relatives. Some historians say he had blue eyes; others say his eyes were brown. But all agree he did not look like a Cherokee; he looked more like a white man. Also, he was a short man, not tall like the ideal warrior. John stood only five feet, six inches tall. Furthermore, he did not speak the Cherokee language fluently. His incapacity with the native Cherokee tongue was a handicap.

The need to communicate may have been one reason John Ross was attracted to Quatie. She a full blood of the Bird Clan, and she had an excellent command of her language. John found a good interpreter in Quatie. Perhaps someone introduced her to him because he needed an interpreter and she could do the job. He may have been impressed with the easy way she spoke two languages.

John was a young, single man. He was looking for help in his work. But he was also hoping to find the right woman to be his wife. John was looking for a woman with depth of character and nobility of mind. Quatie was that kind of woman. She was an attractive woman, too. She was small, probably just over five feet. She had black hair and dark brown eyes. John made a good choice. Quatie would prove her selfless dedication to her people throughout the years.

John Ross and Quatie were married in a ceremony performed at his home near Ooltewah, Tennessee in 1813. It was said that John's marriage to a full blood wife increased his popularity among the Cherokees.

The marriage took place during troubled times. As already stated, the War of 1812 had broken out, and the Cherokees had agreed to help the whites fight against the Creeks. The Cherokees had already refused to join Tecumseh and the Red Sticks. When they heard about the murders at Fort Mims, they joined General Andrew Jackson at Huntsville, Alabama. He was calling for volunteers to fight the Red Sticks. Over 1,000 Cherokee leaders, including John Ross and Junaluska, joined and took part in the battles of Tallushatchie and Talladega. The decisive battle of Tohopeka, or Horseshoe Bend, where the Cherokees were largely responsible for Jackson's success, has been described earlier.

After the War of 1812, John hoped that all would be well for the Cherokee people. He hoped for a time of peace and prosperity. In 1815, John formed a partnership with Timothy Meigs to operate a trading post. It was located at the foot of the present day Market Street in Chattanooga. A ferry was operated across the river. This became known as Ross's Landing, a receiving point for merchandise to be sold at the general store at Rossville. Timothy Meigs died, and Lewis Ross became his brother's new partner. A post office was established at Rossville. John was the first postmaster.

In 1817 John drew up the formal protest stating that the Cherokees wanted no lands in the west but hoped to remain on their eastern lands. He attended the treaty session at Calhoun, Tennessee, in which the U. S. Government asked the Cherokees to cede all lands north of the Hiwassee River and offered inducements for Cherokees to emigrate to the west. That same year John was elected a member of the Cherokee National Council. That was the beginning of his career as a statesman.

Ross served as President of the National Committee from 1819 to 1826. During that time he introduced schools and mechanical training. He directed the development of an autonomous government embodied in the Republican Constitution which was adopted in 1827. Ross was responsible for modeling the Cherokee government into a Republic with a written constitution based on that of the United States.

In 1823, Jackson's two commissioners attempted to bribe the Cherokees into giving up their eastern territory. William McIntosch made a proposition to John based on the argument that the tribes would finally have to sign a treaty anyway. John might as well be paid for negotiating it, he reasoned. The commissioners offered John $2,000 if Chief Ross would persuade his people to agree to the treaty. They would also give $2,000 to the Assistant Chief, Charles Hicks, and another $2,000 to the clerk of the court.

Ross was astonished at such dishonesty. He said that he considered a traitor to be "more despicable than the meanest snake that crawls." He said that he himself would rather live in dire poverty than to have his reputation sullied by the acceptance of a bribe. He told the men that a gross insult had been offered to his character as well as that of the General Council. He said that they had mistaken his character. They had insulted his sense of honor. He was a Christian and would not lower his standards.

When McIntosh was accused by Chief Ross of being a traitor, McIntosh jumped up and rushed out of the room. Ross then suggested that McIntosch not be allowed to attend Cherokee councils ever again. The Council passed this resolution. They expressed their determination to hold no treaties with any Commissioners, and they resolved not to give up even one foot of ground. The resolution passed unanimously. John felt that this meeting and his speech had shown that his people could win through the unity of their actions. He believed their integrity and non-violent methods would win in the end. Because of his reserved but self-confident manner, the admirers of Ross in Washington nicknamed him, "The Indian Prince."

When John Ross was elected principal Chief of the first Indian Republic in 1828, he was thirty-eight years of age. As he stood before the council of the Cherokee Nation at New Echota, the capital, Ross repeated the oath of office. He said: "I, John Ross, do solemnly swear that I will faithfully execute the office of Principal Chief of the Cherokee Nation and will, to be best of my ability, preserve, protect, and defend the Constitution of the Cherokee Nation."

Years later, in 1866, John was 75 years of age and had served his Nation for over fifty years. He said, "I am an old man, and have served my people and the government of the United States. . . over fifty years." He declared that his people had kept him in the harness, "not of my seeking, but of their own choice." He said that he had never deceived them. He also stated that no one in his public life had risen up to upbraid him. "I have done the best I could," he declared.

When Chief Ross died on August 1, 1866, he was satisfied in his own mind that he had kept his oath of office and done his very best with honesty and integrity.

What kind of man, then, did Quatie Ross marry in 1813? He was a man who served as the principal chief of the Cherokee Nation for forty years. He led his people through the most difficult time in their history. He led them through tragic times with courage. Ross helped his Cherokee Nation to create a strong government with a constitution similar to that of the United States. Although he was only one-eighth Cherokee, he felt in his heart more like a Cherokee than a white man. Although he did not speak the Cherokee language, he was able to communicate very well, especially if he had the help of a translator or interpreter such as Quatie.

When gold was discovered on Cherokee land and laws were made to push out the Cherokees, John Ross appealed to the Supreme Court; and he won. But the Court was not obeyed, and the U.S. government sent seven thousand troops to force the Cherokees to move west. Ross made many trips to Washington to try to avoid this tragedy. He knew that he was right and he was very persuasive in his speeches. Yet he was unable to prevent the removal of the Cherokees--an action that resulted in the deaths of nearly one-fourth of the Cherokee Nation

Yet John knew that war with the United States would be futile. He knew it would lead to total annihilation of the Cherokee race. His goal was to preserve the race and to help the people survive, though they had to start over in Oklahoma.

President Abraham Lincoln praised the Cherokee chief when he said that there was only one man in Indian Territory (Oklahoma) "upon whom I now rely for strength and loyalty." He identified that man as John Ross, Chief of Cherokees. Ross was a man struggling to win equal rights for this people through peaceful means. He was a Methodist. He was honest, conscientious, and loyal. He was a great orator and statesman. He was a good diplomat and spokesman.

In his personal life, Ross was a very private man. Whenever possible, he did not allow the world to intrude on his private or family life. When personal problems and sorrows came against him, he kept them to himself. Perhaps that is why so much has been written about his work but so little about his personal life. Much has been recorded about John's business activities, but very little about his family. That is why we know so little about Quatie and not much more about his children. John did not write about Quatie to his business associates. He did not mention his wife in his official letters. He seldom mentioned his children. Yet the events of his life show that he had a very deep love for the mother of his first six children.

CHAPTER 6

The "First Lady" of the Cherokees

When Quatie married John in 1813, life looked good for them. The young couple was hopeful that the disagreements between the Cherokees and the U.S. Government would soon be resolved. When John was elected Chief in 1828, he was, to the Cherokee Nation, like the President of the United States because he was their highest leader. Quatie was, then, the "First Lady," the wife of the Cherokee Nation's greatest leader. Just as the whites had great respect for their President and his wife, so the Cherokee people respected John and Quatie Ross. They wanted them to have the very best. They were pleased that their leader and his wife lived in a big, beautiful, white frame house surrounded by roses.

What kind of "First Lady" was Quatie Ross? She was dedicated to her people and to her family. She was loyal to her husband and helped him in his work, not only by providing her talents as an interpreter and translator, but also by supporting him in his non-violent approach to conflict. She enjoyed making her home beautiful for her husband and her children. She liked cultivating the roses around the Ross mansion. The lawns, the trees, the flowers, and the lovely house made her home a welcome retreat from the cares of the world. The peacocks in the yard were fun to watch and to feed. Quatie must have spent many hours enjoying the sunshine and the shade of the big trees, watching her children play. She took responsibility for the household chores--the cooking, the sewing, the cleaning. But she also took time to teach her children and to play with them. When John was home, Quatie must have spent time discussing the nation's problems with him, listening sympathetically, offering her suggestions, lending her support. Whenever necessary, she employed her language skills to help him in his work.

Quatie loved her home and her children. The six children that she and John had while at the Ross estate--five boys and one girl--were nurtured in a loving environment. The girl was Jennie, sometimes called Jane. The boys were James, Allen, Silas Dean, George Washington, and John Jr. Quatie was the mother of seven children altogether, having given birth to Susan when she was married to Mr. Henley, and then to John's six children.

There was one great sorrow during the time the Ross family was in the Presidential mansion. Quatie and John lost one child, probably soon after birth. Quatie and John must have grieved deeply. The seven children must have stood by sadly as the infant was buried on the grounds of the great Ross estate. Undoubtedly, flowers were planted near the grave site. As stated before, John seldom wrote about his family when composing letters having to do with official business. He always kept his personal life to himself. But of this one great sadness, he made an exception. In a petition to Congress in 1836, John wrote an emotional appeal in an effort to regain his home. (This was after the Ross home had been taken over by the

Georgia State military guard.) He wrote that his home was very important to him. He explained that "the remains of my dear babe" were buried on those grounds. His appeal, as we know, fell on deaf ears.

In spite of all the problems, John and Quatie's children grew up to live successful lives. Except for the child that died at birth, all of Quatie's children lived full and happy lives. In the last years of his life, John took pride in the fact that his daughters were educated and that every one of his sons fought for the Union in the Civil War. John was proud that all his sons served their country in an honorable manner. Susan Henley, Quatie's first child, was so young when her father died that she probably didn't remember him very well. So John Ross, her step-father, was in every way like her own father. Susan married William Shorey Coodey in 1827. He was John Ross's nephew but no relation to Susan since Susan was not John's natural child.

John and Quatie's six children went through the good times and the bad times with the knowledge that their parents would always do their best for them. We do not know a great deal about the children, but we do know when most of them were born, to whom they were married, and when they died.

James McDonald Ross was born in 1814. He married Sarah Mannion. He, like all his brothers, served in the Civil War for the Union. But he was the only one of the Ross brothers to be killed in the conflict. He died of battle wounds in 1864.

Allen Ross, born in 1817, married Jennie Fields. Of all the children, he was probably the closest to his father. After his service in the Civil War, he served as his father's secretary and helped him a great deal.

Jennie or Jane Ross, born in 1821, was the only daughter of John Ross and Quatie. She was educated at the Moravian Female Academy at Salem, North Carolina. She married Return Jonathan Meigs. He was the son of Timothy and Elizabeth Holt Meigs and grandson of Col. Jonathan Meigs. Unfortunately, Jennie's husband Return Meigs was murdered. Jennie, or Jane, as she was called, then married her second cousin, Andrew Ross Nave. Andrew was the son of Susannah Ross Nave (sister of Chief John M. Ross) and Henry Nave. Jennie died in 1894.

Silas Dean or Silas Densmore, was born in 1829. He was named after the United States agent to the Cherokees. After he returned from the Civil War, he married Nannie Rhoda Stiff. They had no children. Nannie died, and then Silas married Jennie Sanders. She died, and Silas then married Elizabeth Raper. He died in 1870.

George Washington Ross, born in 1830, was named after the U.S. President most admired by the Cherokees. He served with the Union Army in the Civil War. He married Nancy Ottolifter in 1850. She died March 8, 1870 and was buried in the old Ross cemetery. George Washington Ross died in 1870.

John Ross, Jr. may be the least well known of the Ross children. In fact, some historians do not list him at all. Others say he died at birth. Yet others list him, stating that John Jr. grew up and married Elizabeth Chouteau. She died, and he then married Louisa Catherine Means.

It is likely that the historians who do not list John Ross, Jr. overlooked him by mistake. For one thing, John Ross named his later son by Mary Bryan Stapler (John's second wife) John Ross, 3rd. It is logical to assume that there must have been a John 2nd (or John Jr.) before John Ross 3rd was born. Thus, we can assume that John Ross, Jr. did exist and was simply overlooked by those historians not mentioning him. All seem to agree that John Ross 3rd, son of Mary Bryan Stapler and John Ross, did exist. And since he was the third to be given the name "John Ross", there must have been an older brother by that name. The older brother was undoubtedly Quatie and John's youngest child. It is not known how long he lived, but since some historians give the name of his wife, he must have lived to adulthood.

Mary Bryan Stapler Ross, the second wife of John Ross, had two children, Annie Bryan Ross, born June 7, 1845 and John Ross 3rd, born in 1847. Annie died October 20, 1876 and never had children. John Ross 3rd married Caroline (Carrie) Cornelison Lazalear. She died June 20, 1894 and John Ross 3rd married again to Christine Hogeland Foreman. Altogether, John Ross had eight children and one step-child(Susan Henley.) Of his own children, six were boys and two were girls. All the children were raised in the Moravian faith. Quatie was a member of the Moravian Church and John was a member of the Methodist Church. Thus, the children were reared with Christian ideals.

Just as some historians say that John Ross had blue eyes and others say he had brown eyes, so there are disagreements among the authorities about Quatie. One writer, an accepted authority on Cherokees, wrote that Quatie did not have much influence on her husband John. One reason given for the argument that Quatie didn't help her husband much is that John never mentioned his wife in over 50 years of his correspondence. However, it must be remembered that John's letters were mainly about official business and not about his personal life.

Some experts say that Quatie was an invalid much of the time and was too weak to do much to help her husband. But she gave birth to eight children, counting the one that died in infancy. She apparently brought up her children in the Christian faith and helped them obtain good educations. She maintained a beautiful home. She showed courage in the face of trouble. She supported her husband in many ways. Hence, she was probably not an invalid, though her health may have been somewhat fragile. We can only speculate as to many of the conditions in the lives of John and Quatie Ross and their children. Historians often disagree as to the impact of various individuals on the events of the day.

Many historians seem to think Quatie was an important influence in

John's life. Some believe that Quatie influenced John's work in important ways. Some historians believe that Quatie was a highly intelligent woman who thoroughly understood the principles, opinions and characteristics of the Cherokees, that she knew the traditions and prejudices of her race, so she was able to help in various communications and negotiations. It is certain that Quatie was the medium through whom Ross communicated with the full bloods. It is known that John did not speak the language of the Cherokees very well. But his wife did. Certainly she must have been a help in translating for him.

In further evidence of Quatie's influence is the testimony of a man who knew John Ross personally very well, Judge John W. H. Underwood. He once stated that John preserved his power and influence due to his wife Quatie's "untiring energy and unbending will." The judge seemed to think that Quatie was a powerful influence and inspiration when it came to her husband's life and work.

Consequently, we can conclude that Quatie must have had a strong influence on her husband. Certainly she was a great assistance to him in many ways. There appears to be enough evidence to infer that Quatie was a powerful influence in John's life. It would seem that she helped him a great deal in his communication with the Cherokees in negotiating with the white U.S. Government officials. She may have acted as an interpreter on certain occasions. Undoubtedly, she gave John insights on the feelings and needs of her people. As a full blood Cherokee, she had better insights as to their ways of thinking and feeling than her husband who was brought up in a white man's world. Like John, she believed in solving problems through peaceful methods. Hence, she assisted John in settling problems peacefully.

CHAPTER 7

Peaceful Protests

John Ross was known for his way of solving problems through peaceful means. He was a man of peace, but he was also a fighter. He had the courage to fight for the rights of his people through legal means, never resorting to violent or illegal methods. John's call for a peaceful end to conflicts was not just motivated by a peace-loving nature, however. He knew that peaceful negotiation was the practical thing to do, that it was in the best interests of his people. He recognized that to fight the entire United States government would mean defeat. Such a fight would end in the total annihilation of the Cherokee race. Other less patient or less foresighted Native American tribes would later prove that to be true. Their efforts to war against the U.S. government were, in the end, futile.

Some men have believed in a cause so strongly that they were willing to go to jail for their cause. In more recent times, Martin Luther King, Jr. was such a man. John Ross was also such a man. In the 1830s, a group of men took a stand for what was right. Some of them were missionaries to the Indians who were wrongfully jailed because of their dedicated work with the Indians. And one of those men, innocently arrested and jailed, was John Ross. In 1835, John Ross took his place along with the other brave men who have suffered behind bars rather than compromise their principles. Through all the turmoil with the whites, John's creed was "no violence." He urged his people to practice non-violence and to maintain their unity. He was determined to overcome the Georgia Indian Codes by peaceful means. In 1832, he thought he had his chance.

The steps leading to the imprisonment of John Ross involve several events. The Georgia legislature had passed a law that would not allow any white man to live among the Cherokees unless he had first taken an oath of allegiance to the laws of the State of Georgia. Most of the missionaries had signed this oath. But a few of them, including Samuel Austin Worcester, refused to sign because they believed that the new laws, the Indian Codes, were not right.

Samuel Austin Worcester was a missionary of the American Board of Commissioners for Foreign Missions, founded by the Congregational church. He had become a missionary in 1825 and had adopted the Cherokee people as his own. He preached to them, taught them, prayed with them, and ministered to the sick. He would not agree to leave them, and he would not agree to sign an oath to uphold laws which were clearly against them. Worcester said that to sign the oath supporting the State of Georgia was to support the newly enacted Indian Codes, which took human rights away from the Cherokees. Consequently, Worcester was jailed and sentenced to four years at hard labor. Other missionaries such as Daniel Butrick and Dr. Elizur Butler were also arrested and jailed. The missionaries felt that the Georgia laws were preventing them from carrying out their work of preaching and teaching the Gospel. They felt that the human rights of the Indians were being violated. Furthermore, they felt that their Constitutional right of freedom of religion was being violated. The Moravians, Baptists, Congregationalists, Presbyterians and Methodists all drew up resolutions in defense of the Cherokees. But the evangelists, including Worcester, were arrested, tried, and convicted of violating the Georgia Codes because they continued to live among the Cherokees without having signed the State oath. Like Paul and other New Testament missionaries, Worcester and Dr. Butler, among others, were put behind bars and chained, either two by two or chained to their bedsteads.

Chief Ross called the Cherokees to a day of fasting and prayer, saying, "We need to go to the Ruler of the universe in this day of deep affliction. We have trusted too long to the arm of flesh." Ross not only wanted to see problems solved peacefully, but he also wanted his people to remain united in their efforts. He knew that they could only win victories for the Cherokee nation if they remained together in their decisions and actions. He knew that if a few Cherokees went their own way, the rest would be in trouble due to a lack of harmony and unity.

When Ross learned that Worcester and the other missionaries had been imprisoned, he was sympathetic, not only for Worcester, but for his wife Ann and their two children. Ann wanted to go and visit her husband. Several men, including Joseph Vann, John Ridge, Captain McNair, George

Lavendar, and John Ross contributed money to send Ann Worcester to Milledgeville to see her imprisoned husband. There was enough money donated to pay for her trip and her return home, plus enough left over to buy a blanket or two for him.

Chief Ross believed that Worcester had been wronged and should not be kept in jail. Ross took legal steps and appealed to the Supreme Court. On March 4, 1832, the Cherokees brought the case of *Samuel A. Worcester vs. The State of Georgia* before the Court. Chief Justice John Marshall of the Supreme Court was highly renowned. He was one of the most well-known and respected men ever to serve on the Supreme Court, the highest court of the land. Justice Marshall ruled that the law by which the missionary Worcester was imprisoned was unconstitutional. He declared that only the federal government, not Georgia, had jurisdiction over the Indian tribe. The Cherokee attorneys had argued that the tribe constituted a separate and sovereign nation and that neither the federal nor state government had the right to impose its laws upon them.

In a land-mark decision, the Supreme Court declared that it had no jurisdiction over this matter because, as Chief Justice Marshall said, "An Indian tribe or nation within the United States is not a foreign nation in the sense of the Constitution." Marshall affirmed the tribe's right. He stated that the Cherokee Nation was a distinct community, occupying its own territory, with boundaries accurately described. He said that the citizens of

Georgia had no right to enter their territory except with permission from the Cherokees themselves, or in conformity with treaties, and with the acts of Congress.

The meaning of the decision for this case went beyond the fact that the missionary Samuel Austin Worcester had been put in jail illegally. The case was really a question of whether the Indian Code laws in Georgia were legal. The question was whether the whites had the right to infringe on Cherokee land. The ruling of the Court also confirmed the fact that the land belonged to the Cherokees and that the U.S. Government had no right to remove the Cherokees from their land. Thus, the decision was the most important court ruling in the history of the Cherokee Nation. The decision showed that the Georgia Codes were illegal.

When Chief Justice John Marshall ruled in favor of the Cherokees and against the Georgians and their Indian laws, Ross and his people were filled with joy. They truly believed the question of right and wrong had been settled forever. After all, the Supreme Court was the highest court in the land. Its word was final. No one could dispute it. So when news of the Supreme Court decision reached the Cherokees, there was a great celebration. It meant that the terrible Georgia Indian Codes were unconstitutional. It meant that the Court recognized that the Georgians were trespassing on Cherokee lands. It meant that the land taken in the Georgia lottery would have to be returned to the original Cherokee owners. Elias

Boudinot, a great Cherokee leader, wrote home to his brother that the laws of the state of Georgia were declared by the highest judicial tribunal in the country to be null and void. He wrote that the question is forever settled as to "who is right and who is wrong."

Indeed, the Court's decision established the right of the imprisoned missionaries to be set free. It declared that the Cherokees had the right to protection from the aggressions of the state of Georgia. The law under which the missionaries had been put in jail had been repealed.

Sometimes when a law is made or declared, however, it is not enforced. Such a thing happened when the Supreme Court ruled that the Cherokees were entitled to their rights. President Jackson's scorn for the Court's decision and for the Court itself was clear in his well-known remark, "John Marshall has rendered his decision; now let him enforce it." Jackson took it upon himself to ignore the Supreme Court ruling. The success of John Ross and his people in arguing their case before the Supreme Court was a success. The fact that Jackson did not enforce the ruling does not change the fact that the Cherokees won their case.

Jackson's only concern was removing the Indians from the land and turning it over to the whites. So while the Indians celebrated the ruling that the Indian Codes were unconstitutional, Georgia authorities ignored the Court's decision. The Court itself had no power to carry out its own decision. That was the duty of the executive branch of government, the

Presidential branch. And President Jackson refused to obey the Court's decision.

Jackson, called "Chicken Snake" by the Cherokees, ignored the Court's decision because he wanted the Cherokees to be moved west across the Mississippi so the white men could have the riches of the land for themselves. So Worcester was kept in jail another year, even though his rights were being violated and the highest court in the land had made it clear that a man had been imprisoned without cause.

Chief Ross's great fear that his people might fail to work in unity and harmony came to pass. In March, 1835, a secret treaty was drawn up without the knowledge of the Cherokees. This treaty was put together by the Ridges and a few other Cherokees. It provided for the cession of all the Nation's lands east of the Mississippi in return for $3,250,000 in lands in Indian Territory. When the others learned what had happened, they were very angry and felt betrayed by their own people. There was talk of killing John Ridge, Elias Boudinot, and others who had drawn up what they called "the dirty paper."

The men wanting to cooperate with the government by signing what became known as the Treaty of New Echota included The Ridge and Elias Boudinot. These men believed that the only way for the Cherokees to survive as a people was to cooperate with the government and move West. They were ready to give up. They became known as The Treaty Party. The other group, including John Ross and the majority of the Cherokees, wanted to continue trying to convince the government to allow the Cherokees to stay and keep their land. They became known as the National Party. They continued to hope that the Supreme Court decision would be enforced. They did not want to give up and move west.

John Ross steered the Cherokee Nation away from violence against itself. He went to Washington after a Council meeting to inform Jackson of the wishes of the majority of the Cherokees. Their wishes, of course, were to remain on their land. But Jackson was determined to force the removal of the Cherokees. Government agents had called a meeting in the capital town of New Echota to explain the treaty once again to the Cherokees. They wanted to obtain their agreement once and for all. Circulars were distributed through all the towns in the Nation. These papers informed people of the meeting and warned that anyone who didn't go to it would be counted as voting in favor of the treaty. But Ross and other anti-treaty leaders stayed away. They wanted to have nothing to do with the government officials and their wrongful deeds in trying to take the Cherokee land. In the end, only three hundred Indians attended the meeting on December 21, 1835. One of them was Major Ridge. The next week, members of the Treaty Party gathered at the home of Elias Boudinot and signed the treaty.

Members of the Treaty Party, including John Ridge, Elias Boudinot, and Charles Vann, felt that it was better to give in to the wishes of the white government officials. They felt it was futile to fight any more. But the majority of the Cherokees felt that all means had not yet been exhausted to try to avoid removal to the west, especially since the Supreme Court had already ruled in their favor.

The members of the Treaty Party agreed to sell Cherokee lands east of the Mississippi River to the United States in return for five million dollars, the cost of removal to the West, and one year's living expenses in their new homes. The men who signed the treaty knew that it was wrong. According to Cherokee law, anyone who sold land without the approval of the Nation would be put to death. Since the treaty had not been approved by most members of the General Council of the nation, it was not lawful. As The Ridge signed the paper, he said, "I have signed my death warrant."

Even though all but a small minority of the tribe had rejected the treaty, it was accepted by the U.S. officials. The Treaty of New Echota went on to the U.S. Senate for ratification. Nearly sixteen thousand Cherokees, almost the whole tribe, signed a petition denouncing the Treaty as a fraud. They thought that their signatures would convince the white men of the truth.

By the terms of the Treaty, the United States agreed to pay three and a quarter million dollars to the Cherokee Nation in return for all Cherokee land east of the Mississippi River. The Indians were to receive land in Indian Territory, what is now Oklahoma. They were given the promise that the western land would never be taken from them against their wishes. One hundred Cherokees, private citizens who were not Council members, signed the treaty. These men were not authorized leaders of the tribe and had no right to sign official treaties. The white government officials knew that the hundred signatures were not those of legislators and that the treaty was not legally ratified. But President Jackson pretended that he had a legal document to act upon.

Many intelligent men in Congress listened to John Ross. Henry A. Wise of Virginia made a speech in the House of Representatives reminding Congressmen that Ross was one of those who swam the river at Horseshoe Bend and helped win a victory for "Andy" Jackson. Yet Ross had now been turned out of his own house by "citizens of a Christian nation," Wise said. Wise stated that John Ross was known by members of the assembly to be an honest, intelligent man, a man worthy to sit in the councils of this nation, "let alone in the councils of an Indian tribe."

Rallies protesting the Treaty of New Echota as a national dishonor were held in many northern cities. Legislators such as New England's Daniel Webster and Tennessee's Davy Crockett spoke against it in Congress. Philosopher Ralph Waldo Emerson, wrote an open letter to President Jackson which told of the outrage much the country felt about the injustice against the Cherokees. But the words of all these well-known men did not persuade the President. Jackson backed the Treaty with all his power.

The Treaty was accepted by the U.S. Senate in spite of Ross' attempts to get it voted down. The amazing fact is that the Senate approved the Treaty <u>by a single fateful vote</u>. This serves of an example of how one vote can make a difference! One man, Senator Hugh Lawson White, cast the single vote that determined the fate of the Cherokee Nation, causing them to be removed by force form their lands.

As soon as he heard the news, John sent word to his people to ignore the illegal treaty. He called it the "Phantom Treaty."

Because of John's activities against the illegal Treaty, he and John Howard Payne were arrested on December 5, 1835. Payne had been interested in the Cherokees and was thinking of writing a history of their nation. John had consented to let him transcribe official Cherokee records. So he had become one of John's friends and advocates. Payne was a famous actor, playwright and writer. He was made famous for the words of his song, "Home, Sweet Home." The Guard took away a manuscript on Cherokee history which Payne had written. They also took John Ross's official papers.

A charge was fabricated or made up against the two men. Twenty-five members of the Georgia Guard took Ross and Payne to Camp Benton and locked them into a dank, dark log cabin which served as a jail. Chained near them was the son of Crawling Snake, speaker of the Council. Hanging from the rafters above them was the decaying body of a Cherokee who had been executed some weeks before but never buried. John and his friend were released 13 days later. No charges had ever been preferred against them.

While John and his friends were persecuted, The Ridges and Boudinot received special consideration by the whites because they had signed the Treaty. The Treaty Party went its own way. They made agreements with the U.S. Government in competition with Ross and against the will of the majority of the Cherokees. They were given three thousand dollars in traveling money by the State. The unity of the Cherokees had been broken. Now Georgia was able to do more against the Cherokee Nation.

Although other leaders, including Major Ridge, Elias Boudinot, and John Ridge, had agreed to cooperate with the government and to move west, John Ross said that the feelings of the majority of the people should always prevail. He said that it was the duty of the minority to yield to the wishes of the majority. But Ridge and the others did not follow the rule of the majority. They felt they had to deceive the people for their own good, so they had made the secret treaty.

Chief Ross was determined to stand up for the rights of his people. He said, "We will not yield one inch of land!" He was willing to fight as many legal battles as he could to keep the U.S. Government from removing the Cherokees from their eastern lands. He had been willing to go to jail, innocent of wrong-doing, in order to peacefully protest what he felt was right. He made a well-known statement: "There are only two ways to end a controversy--a right way and a wrong way."

In 1835, two delegations went to Washington, one led by Ross and the other by Ridge. Ninety percent of the Cherokees stood in favor of what John believed in. They opposed giving up their land in the East. They opposed the illegal Treaty of New Echota. But Jackson refused to meet with the Ross delegation although the President warmly received the Ridge party.

Chief Ross's people obeyed his instructions for peaceful protest and civil disobedience. They refused to give to white census takers the names of their children. They refused to enumerate their farm improvements. They refused to estimate the number of acres they cultivated. They refused to tell officials how many cattle they owned. For failing to do this, both men and women were stripped and beaten by the Georgia Guard.

Their Cherokee lands had been overrun. Their schools had been closed. Their interests had been betrayed. Their unity had been broken. Yet the Cherokees under John Ross tried to remain firm. Ross made many trips to Washington, hoping to persuade the new President Martin Van Buren to reconsider Jackson's previous policy toward the Cherokee Nation. Ross tried to rally Cherokee supporters in the Senate to overturn the Treaty of New Echota legally or to find some other way of allowing his people to retain even a small portion of their land.

Only two thousand Cherokees had voluntarily moved. Among them were the Ridges, Boudinot, and others in the Treaty Party. But the majority of the Cherokee Nation remained. In May, 1838, General Winfield Scott arrived in the Cherokee Nation with seven thousand troops, almost one soldier for every two Indians. His job was to remove the rest of the Cherokee Nation from their lands in the east and take them to western Indian Territory--Oklahoma--by force.

CHAPTER 8

"The Place Where They Cried"

General Winfield Scott threatened the Cherokees and warned them against resisting or running away. He promised them food, clothing, and that they would "at your ease and in comfort, be transported to your new homes." Instead of finding food, clothing, ease, and comfort, however, the Cherokees were herded into pens sixteen feet square, crudely roofed over. They were crowded together, given poor food, and little medical care when they became sick. They were huddled together like animals in a corral.

Chief John Ross now put all of his energy into seeing that his people survived the journey with as little hardship as possible. He appealed to General Scott. The words of Scott's harsh proclamation of May 10, 1838 seemed very stern. It would seem that he would be unwilling to listen to any appeals. Yet, when approached by Ross, he gave him everything he asked for! Ross asked that the soldiers guarding the stockades be removed. He asked that the people be allowed to scatter out and make camp for themselves. He asked that they have medical care. And he asked that their own leaders be allowed to plan and supervise the trip west. Scott respected John Ross and listened to his requests. He granted all of them. He respected Ross so much that he put his military career in jeopardy rather than to see injustice continue. Ross had won a victory in persuading Scott to make conditions better for the people.

It seemed that Chief John Ross' persuasive abilities seldom failed. His Christian sincerity and honesty came through whenever he spoke. The Indians trusted Ross so completely that one unconverted Cherokee told a missionary that if Mr. Ross told him believe the Gospel, he would. It is not known if the Indian was converted, but if he was, it was probably because of the persuasive power of John Ross' oratory.

Chief Ross felt that he had failed, however, in convincing the minority of Indians to stay with the majority in speaking against giving up more land. Thus, Major Ridge, John Ridge, Elias Boudinot and others drew up the secret Treaty of New Echota. Furthermore, Ross failed to convince the authorities that this treaty was not valid. John's petition to Congress showing that the majority of the Cherokees (ninety percent) were not in favor of that Treaty accomplished little. However, men of integrity such as John Quincy Adams, Daniel Webster, and Davy Crockett spoke against the illegal treaty and the removal of the Cherokees.

Ralph Waldo Emerson, a well-known writer, sent a letter to President Martin Van Buren urging him to recognize that the Treaty of New Echota was invalid. He asked the President not to move the Indians from their land. He wrote that the soul of men, the justice, the mercy that is in the heart's heart in all men "does abhor this business." He boldly told the President he would surely bring down that "renowned chair in which you sit into infamy if your seal is set to this instrument of perfidy."

But finally, the Senate ratified the treaty by one vote, as mentioned previously. Most of John Ross' failures were due to his not having a chance to speak--or due to other people and situations beyond his control. Yet the fact that he upheld non-violence while other Indian leaders donned war-paint is commendable. In spite of all efforts, the journey west was a time of trouble and tragedy. Often a gang of roughnecks followed the soldiers to take things from the cabins as soon as the soldiers left. They thought it was all right to steal from the Cherokees. They reasoned that the Indians had no right to be in Georgia in the first place. Soldiers began to seize the Indians as they worked in their homes or fields, giving them no time to gather up anything to take with them.

About one thousand Cherokees refused to be removed and escaped. They lived as fugitives in the Great Smoky Mountains. The rest suffered the fate of the long journey. Chief Ross had to admit there was nothing more he could do to avoid the removal of the Cherokees. Now the only thing to do was to make the best of the bad situation. His goal was to see that his people survived. Sometimes families were separated, never to see each other again. Old or sick people who fell to the ground were dragged to the side of the road and left there to die or to recover alone. Their families were forced to go on without them. Two children ran into the woods to escape the soldiers. Their mother begged to be allowed to go and find them, promising that she would then return to the stockade. But she was driven off with the other prisoners. A confused deaf mute who turned right when ordered to go left was shot and killed for his mistake! An officer in the Georgia militia who took part in the round up wrote that he had fought through the Civil War and had seen men shot to pieces and slaughtered by the thousands. "But the Cherokee removal was the cruelest work I ever knew."

In October of 1838, the Cherokees gathered in Rattlesnake Springs, Tennessee to begin the long, dreaded trip west, even though cold weather was already setting in. Young people were expected to walk much of the 800 miles to their new home. Packs were strapped to their backs. Going Snake, the 80-year-old leader, headed the first detachment on his pony.

The emigrant's physician, Dr. C. Lillybridge, said that the people fell sick to colds, influenza, coughs, pleurisy, measles, diarrhea, fevers, toothache, and wounds from accidents, among other things.

An elderly soldier wrote a letter to his grandchildren on December 11, 1890. He was eighty years old. He said that he had been a Private soldier in the American Army in the year 1838. He said that he could never forget the sadness and solemnity of that morning in October when the Indians were loaded like cattle or sheep in 645 wagons to start toward the west. He remembered that Chief John Ross led in prayer. When the bugle sounded, the wagons started rolling. Many of the children waved good-by to their mountain homes, for they knew they were leaving them forever. Many of the people did not have blankets and many had been driven from home barefooted. He remembered that on the morning on November 17, there was a sleet and snow storm with freezing temperatures. The winter cold lasted from that day until the end of the journey, so that the trail of the exiles was really a trail of death, according to the old soldier. He said that the Indians had to sleep in the wagons or on the ground without fire. As many as twenty-two a night died of cold and exposure or pneumonia due to ill treatment. The picture of 645 wagons lumbering over the frozen ground with their cargo of suffering humanity lingered in the old man's memory. He wrote that "somebody must explain the streams of blood that flowed in the Indian country."

John Ross did his best to help his people keep their courage. On horseback, he cantered up and down the column, checking on details. He shook hands with the leaders of the groups which were about to take off, assured that each knew the route to be followed. The Cherokees made the long trip according to a plan devised by John Ross. He had divided the people into 13 groups, with about one thousand in each group. Each party had elected two leaders. Ross headed the 13th detachment. He rode forward and back along the lines of refugees, watching over the people. He encouraged them as he went, and he directed the line of the march. Quatie and her youngest son rode in a carriage in the Ross detachment. The

Cherokees expected to spend about two and a half months on the road. But the trip was four months long. One detachment spent six months in travel. An unusually severe winter set in during November. Wayside graves became commonplace. The wagons were intended to hold provisions and to store cooking utensils and a few household goods. But the wagons also carried the children, the elderly, and the sick. Soon the wagons were so packed with sick people that household goods had to be thrown out. When sick people lay shoulder to shoulder on the floor of a wagon, even cooking pots and dishes had to be cast away. Food became more and more scarce. After the first detachment went through, there was little game left.

According to Ross, 424 emigrants out of the thirteen detachments died along the journey west in 1838-39. It is estimated that out of the total of 18,000 Cherokees who went west after the Treaty, about 4,000 died, either in stockades before the removal or on the journey west. The last detachment of Cherokees reached Indian Territory (Oklahoma) in the spring of 1839. The route they traveled was known forever after as the Trail of Tears or, in Cherokee, *Nunna-da-ul-tsun-yi*, "The Place Where They Cried."

John Ross managed to carry all the Cherokee records: the letters from Presidents since President Washington, the Cherokee Nation's first written laws, and all the broken and dishonored treaties. Chief John Ross saved the Nation's important papers. But he could not save the one thing which was the most precious to him: the life of his beloved wife.

CHAPTER 9

A Mother's Love

Sleet, snow, and bitter winds assaulted the travelers. It was the end of January. Quatie had been ill for days. Quatie's husband John had ridden ahead to confer with leaders of another detachment.

When they came upon a party with a number of children, Quatie noticed that one of the children was very ill and had no blanket. She gave her own blanket to the child. Later, the child recovered. But Quatie huddled all night in her wagon, wrapped in all the clothing she could find. She shivered in the fierce pounding of icy winds. In a last act of compassion, the sacrifice of a mother's loving heart was evident in Quatie's response to a need.

We do not know what Quatie's last words or thoughts were. So the rest of this chapter is speculation based on the few facts as we know them.

Possibly Quatie's health had been fragile most of her life. Perhaps she had been in poor health for a while. Perhaps no one was especially alarmed when Quatie took a cold. The conditions of the journey, however, made her illness worse. Perhaps Quatie did not want her husband to worry. He had so many important things on his mind. She may have made efforts to conceal the seriousness of her illness, as she wished her husband to continue with his work without worry about her. There was nothing he could do to make her health better, she may have reasoned, so he should not be distracted from his work. Perhaps that is why he left Quatie alone in the wagon that night to ride ahead to another detachment. Perhaps he did not realize how seriously ill Quatie was. Certainly he did not recognize that she was dying.

Quatie and John must have had many long talks about their plans for the future. Once they reached their new home in Oklahoma, they would build a beautiful house, John promised. Quatie probably told John the kind of house she would like to have. Undoubtedly, she told him she wanted the new house to be surrounded by roses likes the old one was.

Maybe at some time during their conversations, the possibility that one of them might not survive the journey occurred. John probably gave Quatie detailed plans as to what she must do to carry on should she be widowed. He probably told her of the importance of preserving the Nation's important papers. Quatie probably told John her wishes should she not survive the journey. But they both made up their minds to do their best to survive and to help their people start a new life in the new land.

Perhaps Quatie reviewed her life as she lay in the grips of the terrible fever. Perhaps she thought of her childhood and her family. Maybe she remembered happy days as she played at her childhood home. She may have remembered falling in love and marrying Mr. Henley. She must have remembered her wedding. And she must have remembered the birth of her first child Susan. She may have thought of her sorrow when Mr. Henley died. She must have remembered the first time she saw John Ross. She must have thought of their courtship and their wedding. She must have remembered the birth of each child. She must have recalled her sorrow at the loss of the child that was buried on the Ross estate. And she probably thought of many happy moments she had shared with her children and her husband.

Maybe she remembered the problems she and John had faced together. She probably remembered how she felt when the white men came and told her that her house was no longer her own home and that she must prepare to leave. She must have remembered the two years she and her family lived in the one-room log cabin while John fought against the Georgia Codes--and won with the Supreme Court decision--only to lose to Jackson's opposing will. She must have thought of the treason of the Cherokees who signed the Treaty of New Echoa illegally. But through it all, she must have thought of how her husband kept up his courage and how she cheered him on and bravely assisted him in every way she could.

Quatie must have felt a warm glow in her heart when she thought of the child whose live she may have saved when she gave up her own blanket. She must have prayed for the future well-being of her children, of John, and of her people. Quatie must have known that she was feverish with pneumonia. The chills and fever must have left her weak, perhaps only half-aware of the sounds of the night outside her wagon. Perhaps the thought of sunshine and roses in the new land gave her comfort. Perhaps she imagined her children gathered around the new house, playing in the tall, green grass under the gentle rays of the sun, hearing the sounds of happy birds and little creatures in the near-by woods. Perhaps she thought of them surrounded by the sweet scent of roses.

    Whatever Quatie thought as she lay dying, certainly her thoughts for her people, for her husband John, and for her seven children were loving, caring thoughts. She must have prayed, as she had learned as a young girl. Quatie was a brave wife and mother, a noble woman whose last magnanimous act exacted from her a heavy cost--the cost of her life.

CHAPTER 10

A Soldier's Midnight Vigil

Some writers report that Quatie died on the riverboat *Victoria* at Little Rock, Arkansas and that John left the boat to bury her in the frozen ground. But most historians agree that she died in a wagon along the trail. It is true that some of the Cherokees did travel by boat, and the Rosses may have been among them at an earlier date; but by February 1, 1839, the day Quatie died, the Ross family was traveling along the wagon trail.

Under the conditions of cold and deprivation, inadequate food and clothing, with continuous travel under adverse conditions, it is hardly surprising that many of the travelers became ill. Quatie was one of those whose health began to suffer along the trail.

Undoubtedly, Quatie fought a fever and prayed for recovery of her health. How long she was sick is not known. Feverish with pneumonia, Quatie died in the still hours of the winter night near Little Rock, Arkansas, February 1, 1839.

Private John Burnett was on guard duty that night. Private Burnett of Captain Abraham McClellan's Company, had been sent to assist in the Cherokee Indian removal. He kept a diary in which he reported his eyewitness accounts of the Great Removal. He spoke the Cherokee language and so was sent as an interpreter into the Smoky Mountain Country in May, 1838. There he witnessed how the Cherokees were arrested and dragged from their homes, driven at the bayonet point into the stockades. He reported that in the chill of a drizzling rain on an October morning, he saw the Indians loaded "like cattle or sheep" into six hundred and forty-five wagons to be taken west.

Burnett wrote in his diary that he could never forget the sadness and solemnity of that morning in October and that Chief John Ross led in prayer. A bugle sounded and the wagons started rolling. Many waved good-by to their mountain homes, knowing they were leaving them forever.

On November 17th, there was a sleet and snow storm. Some of the Indians had no blankets. Others had been driven from their homes barefooted. Freezing temperatures assailed the travelers until they reached the end of the fateful journey on March 26, 1839. It was said that the trail of the exiles "was a trail of death." The people had to sleep in the wagons and on the ground without fire.

Burnett stated that he knew as many as twenty-two of them to die in one night from pneumonia due to ill treatment, cold, and exposure. Among that number, Burnett reported, was the "beautiful Christian wife of Chief John Ross."

Burnett said that "this noble hearted woman died a martyr to childhood, giving her only blanket for the protection of a sick child." He said that Mrs. Ross rode thinly clad through a blinding sleet and snow storm, developing pneumonia, and died in the still hours of a bleak winter night, "with her head resting on Lieutenant Gregg's saddle blanket."

Burnett explained in a diary that he was on guard duty the night Mrs. Ross died. He said that he was relieved at midnight, but he did not retire. He remained around the wagon where Mrs. Ross lay "out of sympathy for Chief Ross." At daylight he was detailed to assist in the burial.

According to Burnett's diary, Quatie's "uncoffined body was buried in a shallow grave far from her native mountain home, and the sorrowing cavalcade moved on."

After Quatie's death, Burnett wrote that he did all that a Private soldier could do to alleviate the sufferings of the people. When he was on guard duty at night, he many times "walked my beat in my blouse in order that some sick child might have the warmth of my overcoat."

Burnett clearly admired Quatie Ross for her sacrifice of her blanket for the sick child, and he himself imitated her actions. Quatie was, even in her last hours, an inspiration to others.

One can only imagine the sorrow facing John Ross the morning after Quatie's death. Additionally, the grief of their children must have been overwhelming. John must have wondered how he was to go on without his wife, without her help and guidance, without her steady hand as a homemaker and mother, as well as a wife, to begin all over in a new place, the land known as Oklahoma, the dreaded place in the west that the

Cherokee nation had resisted for so long. But John knew he had to keep going for his people, for his children, and for the important work to be done in the new home, even though Quatie was no longer going to be a part of it.

CHAPTER 11

A New Hope

The Cherokees surviving the infamous Trail of Tears were willing to start over in the new land. At Park Hill, just outside of Tahlequah, the newcomers constructed Rose Cottage, the palatial estate of John Ross. It was to serve as the "White House" or official residence for the Chief.

It has been said that John Ross had an aristocratic manner. He possessed a regal or king-like grace and dignity befitting the chief of a noble race of people. He had a deep sense of graciousness which gave him the ability to be a good host to all who visited his home. It is ironic that, being more white than Indian, he could have spent his entire life as a white man, could even have denied his Indian blood, and had nothing to do with the tribulations of the Cherokees. But early in life he chose to be Cherokee, and his loyalty never wavered.

It took a while for the Cherokees to settle into their new homes. Many of the settlers blamed the Treaty Party for the suffering they had endured and the loved ones they had lost. They felt they had been betrayed when the men of the Treaty Party split the unity of the Nation and cooperated with the U.S. Government before all efforts had been exhausted in negotiating with the whites.

On June 22, 1839, Major Ridge's fears, expressed when he signed the Treaty of New Echota, came about. He, his son John Ridge, and Elias

Boudinot were murdered. Only Stand Watie, the brother of Elias Boudinot, escaped. Upon hearing of the deaths, several other members of the Treaty Party fled for safety to the protection of the garrison at Fort Gibson. The men were killed in accordance with the law of the Nation, which made it treason, punishable by death, to cede away lands except by act of the general council of the Nation. It was certain that members of the National party were responsible for the deaths of the Treaty Party members.

Some people thought John Ross was responsible for the deaths. Boudinot's brother, Stand Watie, vowed vengeance against John. Some of John's friends urged him to flee for his life. But declaring his innocence, John refused to run. He had always abhorred violence, and he had no part in the murders.

The murders made the division in the Nation worse than ever. Once again, John called for unity and peace. About three weeks later, the National Council passed decrees declaring that the Treaty Party men had rendered themselves outlaws by their own conduct. Amnesty was extended to the others on certain conditions. The slayers were declared guiltless of murder. Finally unity was restored.

Three months later John was elected Principal Chief of the Cherokee Nation in the West. On September 6, 1839, a new constitution was written at Tahlequah. Tahlequah was chosen as the new national capital.

Although John grieved deeply for Quatie, he knew that life had to go on. His deep faith carried him through the most difficult times in his life. He did not want to spend the rest of his days alone. He met a young Quaker lady named Mary Bryan Stabler of Wilmington, Delaware. Born in 1824 in New Castle County, Delaware, Mary came from a prominent and highly respected family. At the age of nineteen, she was a highly accomplished young lady.

John and Mary were married in Philadelphia on September 2, 1844. They lived happily until her death in 1865.

John had already fathered six children. Including his step-daughter Susan Henley, he had reared seven children. But his new wife Mary wanted children of her own. She and John had two children, a girl and a boy.

The oldest of John and Mary's children was Annie Bryan Ross, born June 6, 1845. She was born in Tahlequah District, Cherokee Nation, Indian Territory. She married Leonidas Dobson and died October 20, 1876. She had no children.

The second child of John and Mary was John Ross, 3rd. He was born in 1847 in the Tahlequah District, Cherokee Nation. He attended a boys' academy in Nazareth, Pennsylvania and the Lawrenceville Classical and Commercial High School. He married Caroline or Carrie Cornelison Lazalear who was born May 6, 1846 at Hare's Corner, Delaware. She died June 20, 1894. John then married again. His second marriage was to Christine Hogleland Foreman.

Some sources list a third child born to John and Mary Stabler Ross--Mary. But little is known about her and most historians do not list a third child at all. It could be that a third child, Mary, died at birth.

It is known that a month before his death, Ross made out a final will leaving his real estate in Wilmington to his two children by Mary--Annie and John. He left five thousand dollars to each of his older children.

John Ross's second wife Mary, like Quatie, was in fragile health. John spent much time comforting her, especially since she had been dismissed by the Friends or Quakers when she married outside of her faith. (John was a Methodist, not a Quaker.) Later Mary joined the Methodist church. Her children were baptized in the Methodist faith also. After a long illness, Mary died of lung congestion at the age of 40 on July 20, 1865. She was buried at Wilmington, Delaware in the Stapler family plot.

It has been said that John Ross kept his personal life apart from his business dealings. He was a very private man in that respect. But he had deep feelings for his family. For instance, he always remembered his daughter Annie's birthday, and even during the difficult Civil War years, he found a way to send her gifts.

Years after Quatie's death, her remains were exhumed and reinterred in the Mount Holly Cemetery in Little Rock on a lot of General Albert Pike. Pike had been a close friend of Chief Ross and a member of the same Masonic Order. In 1935, the General Izard Chapter, United Daughters of

1812, placed a monument on the lot to the memory of Quatie.

The above actions seem to discredit historians who have written that Quatie had little influence on her husband and that when she died she was hardly mourned and "largely forgotten." Yet numerous writers have recorded that Ross deeply mourned his wife, as did the entire Cherokee Nation. But they were surrounded by death and grief, and they had little time to stop. They had to hurry on along the trail in order to survive. The exiles died by tens and twenties every day of the journey, but no one could stop except to quickly bury the dead and move on. One historian wrote that there was sorrow when the devoted wife of John Ross passed on, leaving him to go on with the bitter pain of bereavement added to the heartbreak at the ruin of his nation.

A devoted mother and wife, a dedicated member of her Tribe, Quatie had loved her family, her people, and her home. The first home had housed "The Indian Prince" and his lady was beautiful. The second home in Oklahoma would be like the White House in Washington, D.C.--a home for a commander-in-chief. John wanted it to be beautiful as well.

It is not a known fact, but it can be inferred that since Quatie and John's first home was surrounded by roses, John wanted his second home in Oklahoma to be surrounded by roses, too. And because of all the beautiful roses around his home, it became known as "Rose Cottage." It seems that it would have been a fitting memorial to Quatie. Perhaps when Quatie and

John planned for their future home, before leaving the old one or while they were on the trail, they had agreed that there would be many roses. Perhaps when Quatie feared the move west, John would comfort her with the idea that he would plant many roses around the new home. He kept his promise

John Ross has been remembered and respected by many. President Abraham Lincoln called him the most trustworthy man in Oklahoma. He was never known to cheat, to lie, or take bribes, or to use violent methods to achieve his ends.

Quatie Ross has not been so well known. Historians have written very little about her. But she assisted her husband throughout the difficult years before the removal to Oklahoma. She was a good wife and mother. She, like her husband, insisted on unity and peace among her people. She resisted violent methods of attaining her goals, just as her husband did. In the end, she gave up her life because she could go on no more. But her spirit lives on as one of the nobility of a nation that refused to die. Her people survived, and that was her ultimate wish. The little girl born two hundred years ago lived a life that made a difference. No one could wish for more.

THE END

APPENDIX

The following is a summary telling about Quatie Ross:

NAME: Elizabeth Brown Henley Ross - "Quatie", also listed as Elizabeth Brown Henley; Elizabeth Martin Ross and Mrs. John Ross.

MAIDEN NAME: Elizabeth Brown - "Quatie"

ANCESTORY: Cherokee, of the Bird Clan

NAME OF MOTHER: Unknown, Cherokee of the Bird Clan

NAME OF FATHER: Perhaps James Brown, treasurer of the Cherokee Nation. Some historians say she was the daughter of a Scottish trader and the sister of Judge James Brown of the Cherokees or perhaps the daughter of Thomas Brown who owned the ferry at Moccasin Bend on the Tennessee River. She was a full-blooded Cherokee of the Bird Clan.

DATE AND PLACE OF BIRTH: 1791 - Tennessee (Ooltewah, Tennessee)

NAME OF FIRST HUSBAND: Martin (?) Henley

CHILDREN BY FIRST MARRIAGE: One daughter, Susan Henley

DEATH OF FIRST HUSBAND: Approximately 1810

DATE OF MARRIAGE TO JOHN ROSS: 1812

PLACE OF MARRIAGE CEREMONY: Home of her father, James Brown, near Ooltewah, Tennessee

NUMBER OF CHILDREN SURVIVING INFANCY: Seven - (1 girl by Henley; 1 girl and 5 boys by Ross)

NAMES OF CHILDREN OF QUATIE: Susan Henley, James McDonald Ross, Allen Ross, Jeannie or Jane Ross, Silas Dean or Silas Dinsmore Ross, George Washington Ross and John Ross, Jr.

RELIGION: Moravian Church, "Christian"

EDUCATION: unknown; probably little formal education but she was fluent in English as well as the Cherokee language.

ACCOMPLISHMENTS: Assisted John Ross in diplomatic communications with the Cherokees; excellent translator; inspired confidence and admiration; probably influenced Ross's non-violent approach

CHARACTER TRAITS: selfless dedication to her people; noble-hearted; beautiful, Christian wife; probably quiet and unobtrusive, strong-willed, intelligent, compassionate, a good mother; loved her husband, her children, her people, her home.

DESCRIPTION OF HOME: A white frame house at the head of the Coosa River in Georgia; well-furnished. On the lawn the Rosses kept a pair of peacocks. There were many roses. When the Ross house was drawn in Georgia's lottery by James Jones and taken over, Ross took his ousted family to Tennessee and built a rough one-room log cabin at "Red Hill" or Flint Springs, near Red Clay Council Grounds; this was Quatie's last home.

DATE OF DEATH: February 1, 1839

CAUSE OF DEATH: Pneumonia

CIRCUMSTANCES LEADING TO DEATH: Exposure to cold on the journey west (The Trail of Tears.) Her health was frail to begin with. She noticed a sick Cherokee boy with no blanket. She gave the child her own blanket, though she herself suffered from illness. The child recovered and survived. Quatie developed pneumonia and died.

PHYSICIAN IN ATTENDANCE: None. (Dr. C. Lillybridge was the emigrants' physician but was not present.)

PLACE OF DEATH: Near Little Rock, Arkansas, on a bluff above the Arkansas River, alone in a wagon "with her head resting on Lieutenant Gregg's saddle blanket."

HONOR GUARD: Private John Burnett

TYPE OF BURIAL: Brief ceremony detailed by Captain Abraham McClellan, the morning following Quatie's death; body was uncoffined, buried in a shallow grave by the roadside near Little Rock.

LATER BURIAL: Quatie's remains were exhumed and reinterred in the Mount Holley Cemetery, Little Rock, on a lot of General Albert Pike, a close friend of John Ross and a member of the same Masonic Order.

EPITAPH: In 1939, the General Izard Chapter, United Daughters of 1812, placed a monument on the lot, west of the monument raised by Pike, to the memory of Quatie Ross: "Quatie; Indian Wife of John Ross; Chief of Cherokee Tribe; Died in Little Rock, Ark.; February 1, 1839."

BIBLIOGRAPHY

Clark, Electa. *Cherokee Chief: The Life of John Ross.* London: Crowell-Collier Press, 1970.

Collier, Peter. *When Shall They Rest? The Cherokee's Long Struggle with America.* N.Y.: Holt, Rinehart, and Winston, 1973.

Fleischmann, Glen. *The Cherokee Removal, 1838.* N.Y.: Franklin Watts, Inc., 1971.

Foreman, Grant. *Indian Removal.* Norman: University of Oklahoma Press, 1956.

Harrell, Sara Gordon. *John Ross: The Story of an American Indian.* Minneapolis: Dillon Press, Inc., 1979.

King, Drane. *The Cherokee Indian Nation: A Troubled History.* Knoxville: The University of Tennessee Press, 1979.

Ruskin, Gertrude McDaris. *John Ross, Chief of an Eagle Race.* Chattanooga, Tennessee: John Ross House Association, 1962.

Schoolcraft, Henry Rowe. *History of the Indian Tribes of the United States: Their Present Condition and Prospects and A Sketch of Their Ancient Status.* Philadelphia: J. B. Lippincott and Company, 1957.

Van Deusen, Glendon. *The Jacksonian Era: 1818-1848.* N.Y.: Harper & Row, Publishers, 1959.

Wilkins, Thurman. *Cherokee Tragedy: The Story of the Ridge Family and of the Decimation of a People.* N.Y.: The Macmillan Company, 1970.

Woodward, Grace Steele. *The Cherokees.* Norman: University of Oklahoma Press, 1963.

www.ingramcontent.com/pod-product-compliance
Lightning Source LLC
Chambersburg PA
CBHW070326100426
42743CB00011B/2579